Pool
Design

teNeues

Editor in chief: Paco Asensio

Editorial and project coordination, texts: Haike Falkenberg

Art director: Mireia Casanovas Soley

Layout: Pilar Cano

Text Natural Pools: Julia Clare for Terravita Gardens

Copy-editing: Raquel Vicente

Spanish translation: Almudena Saisian (Introduction, Natural Pools)

French translation: Marion Westerhoff (Introduction), Michel Ficerai (Natural Po

English translation: Robert J. Nusbaum (Introduction)

Published by teNeues Publishing Group

teNeues Publishing Company
16 West 22nd Street, New York, NY 10010, US
Tel.: 001-212-627-9090, Fax: 001-212-627-9511

teNeues Book Division
Kaistraße 18
40221 Düsseldorf, Germany
Tel.: 0049-(0)211-994597-0, Fax: 0049-(0)211-994597-

teNeues Publishing UK Ltd.
P.O. Box 402
West Byfleet
KT14 7ZF, Great Britain
Tel.: 0044-1932-403509, Fax: 0044-1932-403514

www.teneues.com

ISBN: 3-8238-4531-4

Editorial project: © 2003 **LOFT** Publications

Via Laietana, 32 4º Of. 92
08003 Barcelona, Spain
Tel.: 0034 932 688 088
Fax: 0034 932 687 073

e-mail: loft@loftpublications.com
www.loftpublications.com

Printed by: Gràfiques Ibèria S.A. Barcelona

Pool
Design

■ What do men, melons and swimming pools have in common? They're primarily composed of water. But while people are designed by the forces of nature in an almost endless variety of forms and types, swimming pools are created by architects, landscape architects and the like. In this process, customer's requirements, specialized knowledge and design ideas are merged with water and a piece of property to create a refreshing oasis.

Water has a very special effect on people. Having water to drink is a matter of survival, and we also use it for personal hygiene, as a source of energy, as a means of transportation, as a carrier of nutrients, for play, and just to look at. Water has a restorative effect on both the body and soul. You don't to have spent years practicing meditation in order to go into a deep reverie while contemplating the still, reflective surface of a sheet of water. Shifting sunlight and cloud formations accentuate this everyday, gratis spectacle until the borderline between sky and earth, depth and surface appear to dissolve in the dusk.

Water also allows us to feel weightless when we float or play in it or when ocean swells bear us high in the air. Exercise is good for the limbs and burns more calories than the same movements performed out of the water. Swimming and diving are top priorities for many people of all ages and every summer many of us frolic in rivers and lakes, in the ocean and, yes, in swimming pools.

Today, swimming pools can take on just about any form. Whether the architect inserts in the plan an elongated turquoise blue shape that is bordered by a right angle; or integrates into the topography a round, oval or elliptical mirror-like object; or designs an L-shaped, T-shaped or irregularly shaped pool to make a client's dream come true; in every case there has to be enough horizontal and vertical space, as well as a watertight material that prevents the water in the pool from seeping out.

In choosing the materials for swimming pools, the climate, the way the pool will be used, its shape and depth and its filter system must all be taken into consideration. The materials available range from traditional tiles in every conceivable size, to wear resistant films, preformed fiberglass or metal shells, and stone, concrete and cement. Pools built without seams are generally more watertight and easy to clean. Small mosaic tiles can fit the most challenging contours and do not fragment like their larger counterparts on whose broken edges people can easily injure themselves.

There are also spectacular looking swimming pools with overflow systems in which the water rises to the same level as the border channeling it over the edge of the pool into the recirculation system. Other possibilities include runoff systems with various types of ridges around the edges of the pool or runoff systems that are out of sight under the water. Modern technology also provides a broad range of filters and water recirculation systems, which means that owners can decide which type of water they'd like in their pool: chlorinated, non-chlorinated or even salt water. Swimming ponds, which are becoming increasingly popular, are briefly covered in the final chapter of this book.

When a swimming pool is designed, its depth and slope must be defined. For athletic swimming a long pool is needed and perhaps even a countercurrent device; for a diving board—positioned in such a way that the diver isn't blinded by the sun—of course a basin of sufficient depth. Massage heads and a jacuzzi connected to the swimming pool are beneficial to both body and soul. A clearly visible, separable and safe area should be provided for children. Entry to the pool can be via a space saving ladder or a more comfortable staircase. Both elements have a considerable effect on the overall design of the pool and should be selected with care. The pool area itself should be sunny and protected against prying eyes, and there should be no trees over the pool that lose their leaves in the autumn or plants that attract insects. In some climates, the water in the pool may have to be covered to prevent damage and to keep the water clean.

No matter what size and shape a pool may be, if it is well taken care of and blends well into the surroundings it will act as a restorative to flesh and spirit and can even be a source of inspiration, as the examples in this book. ■

■ Was haben der Mensch, Melonen und Swimming Pools gemeinsam? Sie bestehen zum überwiegenden Teil aus Wasser. Jedoch werden erstere von der Natur in einer nahezu unermesslicher Formen- und Typenfülle modelliert, während für Swimming Pools Architekten, Landschaftsplaner und andere Profis verantwortlich sind. Kundenwünsche, Fachwissen und Design vereinigen sich mit einem Stück Landschaft und Wasser zu wahren Oasen der Erquickung.

Wasser in jeder Form übt auf den Menschen einen besonderen Reiz aus. Als Trinkwasser sichert es unser Überleben, und wir brauchen es zum Reinigen, als Energiequelle, Transportmittel und Nahrungslieferant, zum Spielen und Betrachten. Wasser erfrischt Körper und Geist. Man muss nichts über Meditation wissen, um beim Anblick einer stillen, spiegelnden Wasseroberfläche die Gedanken in die Tiefe sinken zu lassen. Der wechselnde Sonnenstand sowie Wolkenformationen am Himmel akzentuieren dieses alltägliche, kostenlose Schauspiel, bis sich in der Dämmerung schließlich die Grenzen von Himmel und Erde, Tiefe und Oberfläche aufzulösen scheinen.

Wasser lässt uns für Momente die Schwerkraft vergessen, wenn wir den „toten Mann" machen tauchend Kapriolen schlagen oder im Meer von Wellen gewiegt werden. Bewegung im Wasser schont die Gelenke und verbrennt mehr Kalorien, als die gleichen Übungen auf dem Trockenen Schwimmen, baden und planschen stehen ganz oben auf der Prioritätenliste von Jung und Alt – und jeden Sommer tummeln sie sich erneut an Seen und Flüssen, am Meer und in Schwimmbädern.

Swimming Pools können heutzutage eine schier unbegrenzte Anzahl Formen annehmen. Ob der Architekt einen langgezogenen, durch rechte Winkel begrenzten azurblauen Strich in die Landschaft malt, sich eine runder, ovaler oder elliptischer Spiegel in die Topografie einpasst, ein Eigentümer sich einen L-förmigen, T-förmigen oder unregelmäßigen Pool-Traum erfüllt, stets benötigt man einen gewissen Platz, ein Minimum an Tiefe und ein wasserundurchlässiges Material welches das wertvolle Nass am Versickern hindert.

Bei der Wahl der Baustoffe ist das Klima zu berücksichtigen, die Nutzungsweise des Pools, seine Form und Tiefe sowie das Filtersystem. Die Bandbreite der Materialien reicht von der klassischen

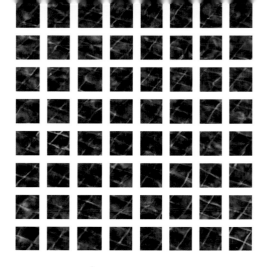

Fliese in den verschiedensten Größen über widerstandsfähige Folien, vorgeformte Hartschalen aus Kunstfasern oder Metall bis hin zu Stein, Zement und Beton. Fugenlose Konstruktionen garantieren im Allgemeinen eine größere Dichte und sind leicht zu reinigen. Kleine Mosaikfliesen können sich den gewagtesten Kurven anpassen und bersten nicht wie ihre großformatigen Verwandten, an deren Bruchstellen man sich schneiden könnte.

Spektakulär wirken Swimming Pools mit Überläufen, bei denen die Wasseroberfläche erhöht liegt und das Wasser zur Aufbereitung über den Rand einer Seite abfließt; andere Möglichkeiten sind mit verschiedenen Rillenformen in die Umrandung oder unter der Wasseroberfläche eingelassene Ablaufsysteme. Die heutige Technik bietet verschiedenste Filter- und Wasseraufbereitungssysteme, so dass man sich auch über die Frage Gedanken machen sollte, welches Wasser es denn sein soll – gechlortes, reines Süß- oder gar Meerwasser. Den immer beliebteren Schwimmteichen widmet sich ein eigenes, kurzes Kapitel am Ende des Buches.

Vor dem Bau sollten die Beckentiefe und der Einstieg definiert werden: Sportliches Schwimmen braucht Länge, vielleicht sogar eine Gegenstromanlage; ein Sprungbrett – so angebracht, dass die Sonne nicht blendet – selbstverständlich eine ausreichende Wassertiefe. Massagedüsen oder an den Swimming Pool angeschlossene Whirlpools sorgen für ein Extra an Erholung. Für kleinere Kinder sollte ein gut einsehbarer, abtrennbarer und sicherer Bereich vorgesehen werden. Der Einstieg kann über eine platzsparende Leiter erfolgen oder über die bequemere Treppe; beide Elemente können das Design des Pools erheblich beeinflussen und sollten daher mit Bedacht gewählt werden. Die Lage sollte blickgeschützt und sonnig sein, ohne laubabwerfende Bäume und insektenanlockende Blumen. Je nach Klima muss das Wasser in der kühleren Jahreszeit abgedeckt werden, um Schäden und Verschmutzungen zu vermeiden.

In welcher Gestalt und Größe auch immer, ein gepflegter Pool, der harmonisch in seine Umgebung eingebettet ist, erquickt den Körper und belebt den Geist und kann ebenso Quelle der Inspiration sein, wie die auf den folgenden Seiten vorgestellten Beispiele. ■

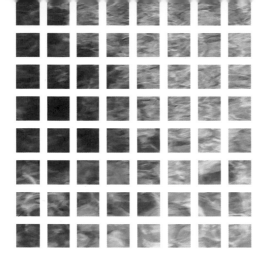

■ Qu'y a-t-il de commun entre l'homme, les melons et les piscines? C'est l'eau car ils en sont tous en grande partie constitués. Toutefois les deux premiers sont façonnés par la nature en une myriade de formes et d'espèces différentes alors que les piscines sont l'œuvre d'architectes, de paysagistes et autres professionnels en la matière. Rêves de clients, experts et design s'harmonisent sur une parcelle de paysage et d'eau pour la métamorphoser en véritable oasis de détente.

L'eau sous toutes ses formes a toujours intéressé et fasciné l'homme. L'eau potable assure notre survie. Sans elle on ne pourrait ni se laver ni nettoyer. C'est une source d'énergie, un moyen de transport et la base de toute nourriture. Elle est tour à tour jeu ou contemplation, un rafraîchissement pour le corps et l'esprit. Même sans être enclin à la méditation, il est facile de plonger dans ses pensées à la vue d'une eau calme et miroitante. Ce spectacle gratuit, quotidien est accentué par les caprices du soleil et les allées et venues des nuages dans le ciel jusqu'au crépuscule où ciel et terre, profondeurs et surfaces semblent se confondre et se dissoudre.

Grâce à l'eau, il nous arrive d'en oublier la pesanteur lorsque nous faisons "la planche", des cabrioles en plongeant ou en nous laissant porter par la mer. Faire des mouvements dans l'eau protège les articulations et fait brûler davantage de calories. Pour les jeunes comme pour les plus âgés, nager, se baigner et barboter sont en tête de liste des priorités. Et chaque été, tout un chacun s'ébat au bord des lacs et des rivières, dans la mer ou les piscines.

De nos jours, les piscines peuvent revêtir mille et une formes. Vue par l'architecte, elle se métamorphose en un long trait bleu azur dans le paysage arrêté en angle droit ou en un miroir rond, ovale ou elliptique intégré à la topographie. Pour réaliser le rêve de son propriétaire, elle épouse la forme d'un L, d'un T ou tout autres contours imaginaires. Quelque en soit le dessin, il faudra toujours disposer d'un certain espace, d'un minimum de profondeur et d'une matière étanche empêchant l'eau si précieuse de s'évanouir dans la nature.

Climat, utilisation de la piscine, forme, profondeur et système de filtrage ont une influence sur le choix des matériaux. L'éventail du matériel s'étend du carrelage classique de formats diffé- rents aux liners résistants en passant par les coques en polyester ou en métal jusqu'aux pier- res, ciment et béton. Les constructions sans joints garantissent une plus grande étanchéité et sont faciles à nettoyer. Les petits carreaux de mosaïque peuvent épouser les courbes les plus osées et ne se fendillent pas comme les grands évitant les blessures éventuelles.

Les piscines à débordement sont spectaculaires lorsque la surface de l'eau surélevée déborde sur un côté avant de retourner dans le système de filtrage. D'autres modèles sont dotés de can- nelures tout autour du bord ou de systèmes d'écoulement sous la surface de l'eau. La technique actuelle offre plusieurs systèmes de filtrage et de préparation de l'eau. La question est donc de savoir quelle qualité d'eau utiliser: l'eau chlorée, douce ou de mer. Nous consacrons un chapi- tre entier à la fin du livre au grand favori du moment, l'étang-piscine.

Avant la construction de toute piscine, il faut en définir l'accès et la profondeur du bassin. Les nageurs sportifs aimeront une piscine longue avec éventuellement une installation à contre-cou- rant; un plongeoir placé en fonction du soleil pour ne pas éblouir bien entendu a besoin d'une profondeur adéquate. Jets de massages ou bains à bouillonnement intégrés à la piscine, sont le summum de la détente. Pour les petits enfants, un petit bain bien séparé et sécurisé est indispensable. L'accès peut se faire grâce à une échelle qui prend peu de place ou par un esca- lier plus commode. Ce sont deux éléments qui peuvent jouer un grand rôle dans le design de la piscine et qu'il faut choisir à bon escient. L'endroit élu doit être à l'abri des regards et ensoleillé, sans arbres à feuilles caduques ni fleurs qui puissent attirer les insectes. Selon les climats et la fraîcheur de certaines saisons, la piscine devra être couverte afin d'éviter salissures et dété- riorations éventuelles.

Indépendamment de sa forme et de sa taille, une piscine doit être en harmonie avec son envi- ronnement afin de vivifier le corps et l'esprit. Elle peut être aussi source d'inspiration comme les exemples suivants. ■

■ ¿Qué tienen en común las personas, los melones y las piscinas? Que están formados en su mayor parte por agua. Sin embargo, la naturaleza modela los dos primeros en una casi infinita variedad de formas y tipos, mientras que de la conformación de las piscinas se encargan arquitectos, paisajistas y otros profesionales. Los deseos de los clientes, la técnica y el diseño se unen en una pequeña parcela de paisaje y agua para formar un oasis de recreo, un remanso de paz para los sentidos.

El agua, en todas sus representaciones, ha ejercido siempre una fascinación especial sobre el ser humano. La ingestión del líquido nos asegura la supervivencia y, asimismo, la utilizamos para lavar, para producir energía, como medio de transporte y como importante fuente de alimentos, para jugar en ella, o simplemente para mirarla y admirarla. El agua refresca el cuerpo y la mente. No hay que saber mucho sobre meditación para ensimismarse contemplando su tranquila superficie de espejo. Los cambios de la posición del sol y las formaciones de nubes en el cielo acentúan este espectáculo diario y gratuito hasta que finalmente, al anochecer, las fronteras entre cielo y tierra, entre profundidad y superficie parecen diluirse.

El agua nos hace olvidar por unos momentos la ley de la gravedad cuando hacemos el muerto en su superficie, damos cabriolas al bucear o nos dejamos mecer por las olas del mar. Nadar, bañarse, chapotear son actividades que hacen las delicias de niños y mayores, y cada verano volvemos a acudir gozosos a lagos y ríos, al mar y a las piscinas.

Hoy en día, las piscinas adoptan una variedad de formas prácticamente ilimitada. Pero independientemente de que los arquitectos dibujen en el paisaje una franja azul alargada y rectilínea, o inserten un espejo redondo, oval o elíptico en la topografía; o si un propietario cumple un sueño en forma de L o de T, o por el contrario, de silueta indefinida, en todos los proyectos se necesita cierto espacio, un mínimo de profundidad y un material impermeable que impida que se pierda el valioso líquido.

En la elección de los elementos de construcción hay que tener en cuenta factores como el clima, el uso que se va a hacer de la piscina, la forma, la profundidad así como el sistema de filtrado.

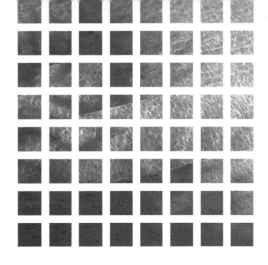

La variedad de materiales abarca desde los clásicos azulejos de diferente tamaño, pasando por resistentes recubrimientos plásticos y formas rígidas prefabricadas en plástico o metal, hasta la piedra, el cemento o el hormigón. Las construcciones sin junturas suelen garantizar la estanquidad, y se limpian fácilmente. Por otro lado, las pequeñas teselas que forman mosaicos se adaptan perfectamente a la curvas y no se resquebrajan como sus hermanas mayores, que pueden cortar con sus aristas.

Especialmente espectaculares resultan las piscinas con rebosadero, en las que la superficie queda algo elevada y el agua cae por uno de los lados para su filtrado; otras están dotadas para ello de acanaladuras en los bordes o de circuitos de desagüe sumergidos. La técnica ofrece actualmente numerosas posibilidades de acondicionar sistemas de filtrado y depuración, por lo que también hay que tener en cuenta el tipo de agua que se va a clorar, agua dulce o del mar. Al final del libro se dedica asimismo un breve capítulo al cada vez más apreciado estanque.

Antes de proceder a la construcción de una piscina hay que determinar la profundidad y el acceso. La natación deportiva necesita determinada longitud, quizás incluso un dispositivo de contracorriente; un trampolín colocado de forma que el sol no deslumbre al saltador, por supuesto, la profundidad necesaria. Además, los chorros y las toberas de masaje y los jacuzzis ayudan a la relajación. Hay que prever también zonas visibles especiales para los niños pequeños, que se puedan separar, y que resulten seguras. El acceso al agua puede llevarse a cabo por medio de escalerillas que ahorran espacio o por cómodas escaleras. Ambos elementos influyen notablemente en el diseño de la piscina y, por ello, deben elegirse cuidadosamente. El lugar de emplazamiento, por otra parte, debe estar protegido de las miradas externas y ser soleado, libre de árboles que dejen caer sus hojas en el agua y lejos de flores que atraigan a los insectos. Según sea el clima, la piscina debe cubrirse durante las estaciones frías para evitar que sufra daños y se ensucie.

Independientemente de la forma y el tamaño, una piscina cuidada e integrada de forma armoniosa en el entorno refresca la mente y reconforta el espíritu, e incluso puede convertirse en una inagotable fuente de inspiración, como los ejemplos en las páginas que siguen. ■

Morabito House

Design: **Jacqueline Morabito**
Location: **Nice, France**
Photos: © **Pere Planells**

Vertical green

Grün vertikal

Vert vertical

Verde vertical

- White tinted cement

- Weiß gefärbter Zement

- Ciment tinté blanc

- Cemento tintado blanco

La Maison des Rêves

Architect: **Thierry Teyssier**

Location: **Skoura Oasis, Morocco**

Photos: **© Pere Planells**

Reflected secret

Spiegelndes Geheimnis

Le miroir aux secrets

Secreto reflejado

- Zellige (terracotta tiles)

- Zellige (Terrakotta-Kacheln)

- Zellige (carreau de terre cuite)

- Zellige (baldosas de terracota)

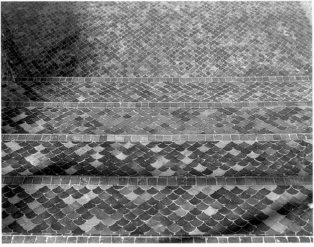

Key Biscayne Residence

Architect: **Laure de Mazieres**
Location: **Miami, USA**
Photos: **© Pep Escoda**

Green-black beauty
Grün-schwarze Schönheit
Beauté verte-noire
Belleza verde-negro

- Black glass mosaic

- Schwarze Glas-Mosaikkacheln

- Mosäique en verre noire

- Gresite de vidrio negro

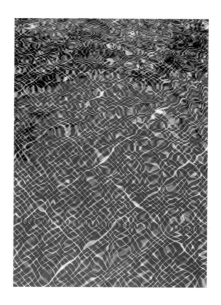

Rustic Contemporary

Architect: **Ramón Esteve**

Furniture: **Ramón Esteve for Gandia Blasco S.A.**

Location: **Ontinyent, Spain**

Photos: **© Pere Planells**

Purity of lines
Die Reinheit der Linien
La pureté des lignes
La pureza de las líneas

- Vaporized ecological pinewood
  Stone-colored mosaic tiles

- Dampfimprägniertes Öko-Kiefernholz
  Steinfarbene Mosaikkacheln

- Bois de pin écologique vaporisé
  Mosaïque en couleur pierre naturel

- Madera de pino ecológico vaporizado
  Gresite color piedra

Riad Kaïss

Design: **Christian Ferré**
Location: **Riad Kaïss,**
Marrakesh Medina, Morocco
Photos: **© Pere Planells**

Waves in the sky

Wellen im Himmel

Des vagues dans le ciel

Olas en el cielo

- Green and white marble powder
  ("Mosaïque")

- Grüner und weißer Marmorpuder
  ("Mosaïque")

- Poudre de marbre verte et blanc
  ("Mosaïque")

- Polvo de mármol verde y blanco
  ("Mosaïque")

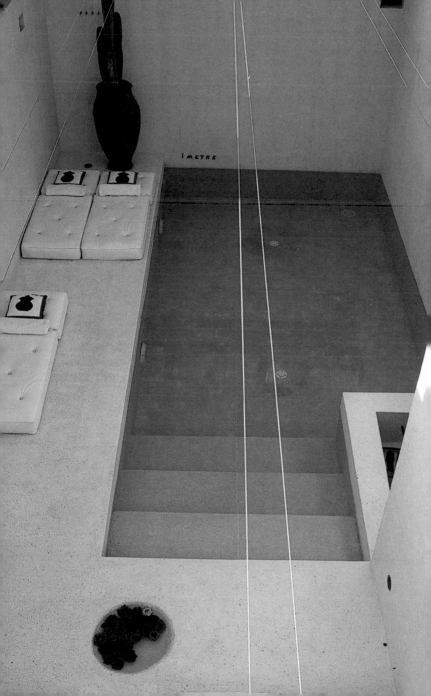

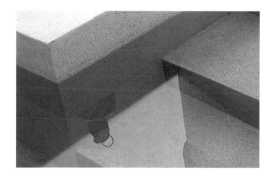

Country Simplicity

Architect: **Alain Houtsaeger**

Location: **Haute Provence, France**

Photos: © **Pere Planells**

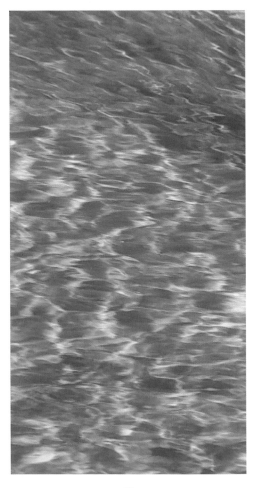

The course of the water
Der Weg des Wassers
Le chemin de l'eau
El camino del agua

- Concrete structure
  Lime rendering
  Natural colorwash
  Grey resin rendering

- Betonstruktur
  Kalkverputz
  Natürliche Farbtünche
  Graue Harzbeschichtung

- Structure en béton
  Enduit en chaux
  Badigeon naturel
  Couverture en résine gris

- Estructura de hormigón
  Revestimiento de cal
  Enlucido natural
  Revestimiento de resina gris

Village House

Architect: **Javier Clarós**
Design: **Eduard Arruga**
Landscape architect: **Pepote Comella**
Location: **Begur, Spain**
Photos: **© Pere Planells**

At the foot of the castle
Zu Füßen der Burg
Au pied du château
Al pie del castillo

- Tinted cement
  Natural stone
  Terracotta tiles

- Gefärbter Zement
  Naturstein
  Terrakottafliesen

- Ciment tinté
  Pierre naturel
  Carrelage de terre cuite

- Cemento tintado
  Piedra natural
  Baldosas de terracota

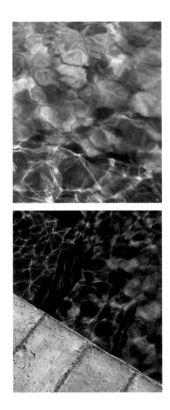

Traditional Style

Architect: **B,B&W Estudio de Arquitectura,
Sergi Bastidas & Wolf Siegfried Wagner**
Location: **Mallorca, Spain**
Photos: © **Pere Planells**

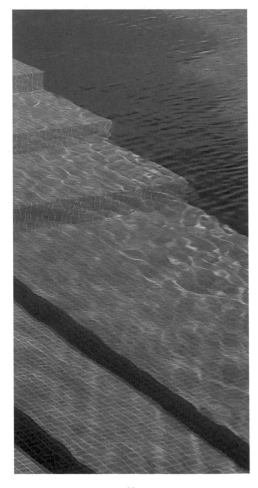

The sky is the limit

Der Himmel ist die Grenze

Le ciel est la limite

El cielo es el límite

- Natural stone
  Green mosaic tiles
  Lawn

- Naturstein
  Grüne Mosaikkacheln
  Rasen

- Pierre naturel
  Mosaïque verte
  Gazon

- Piedra natural
  Gresite verde
  Césped

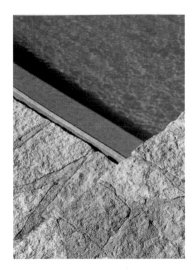

Amidst Windmills

Pool and garden design: **Alvaro de la Rosa**
Location: **Mallorca, Spain**
Photos: © **Pere Planells**

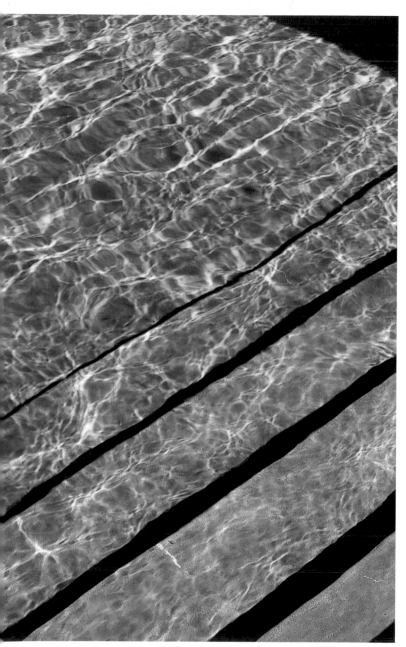

Smooth inclination
Sanfter Anstieg
Douce inclinaison
Subida suave

- Polished cement
  Natural stone from Santanyí
  Tinted cement

- Polierter Zement
  Naturstein aus Santanyi
  Gefärbter Zement

- Ciment ponçé
  Pierre naturel de Santanyi
  Ciment tinté

- Cemento pulido
  Piedra natural de Santanyi
  Cemento tintado

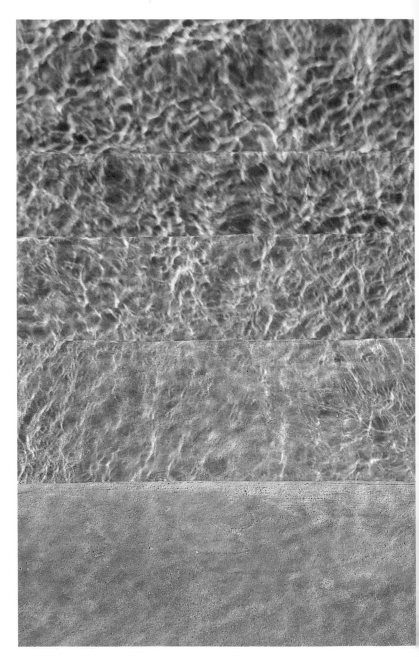

Jnane Tamsna

Pool and garden design: **Meryanne Loum-Martin & Gary Martin**
Location: **Jnane Tamsna Douar Abiad Marrakesh, Morocco**
Photos: © **Pere Planells**

Amidst 1001 palm trees
Zwischen 1001 Palmen
Entre 1001 palmiers
Entre 1001 palmeras

- White ceramic tiles
  Sandy cement

- Weiße Keramikfliesen
  Sandfarbener Zement

- Carrelage en céramique blanche
  Ciment couleur sable

- Baldosas de cerámica blanca
  Cemento tintado color arena

Artist's Home

Design: **Gilbert Herreyns**
Location: **Ibiza, Spain**
Photos: © **Pere Planells**

Natural integration
Natürliche Integration
Intégration naturelle
Integración natural

■ Marès-stone
White mosaic tiles
Pebbles

■ Marès-Stein
Weiße Mosaikkacheln
Kieselsteine

■ Pierre de Marès
Mosaïque blanche
Galets

■ Marès
Gresite blanco
Cantos rodados

Island Home

Pool design: **Renaud Bossert**

Garden design: **Caty Heunoumont**

Location: **Ibiza, Spain**

Photos: **© Pere Planells**

Infinite terraces

Unendliche Terrassen

Terrasses infinies

Terrazas infinitas

- Tinted cement
  Natural stone
  Wood from tropical forests

- Gefärbter Zement
  Naturstein
  Tropenholz

- Ciment tinté
  Pierre naturele
  Bois tropicale

- Cemento tintado
  Piedra natural
  Madera tropical

Le Jas de l'Ange

Architect: **Gérard Gay**

Location: **Orgon, Les Alpilles, France**

Photos: **© Pere Planells**

A custom-made lake
Ein See nach Maß
Un lac sur mesure
Un lago a medida

- Concrete structure
  Sand mixed with resin
  Rocks covered with resin

- Betonstruktur
  Sand-Harz-Gemisch
  Mit Harz behandelter Fels

- Structure en béton
  Sable melangé avec de la résine
  Rocher résiné

- Estructura de hormigón
  Arena mezclada con resina
  Rocas tratadas con resina

Le Mas des Câpriers

Design: **Christine & Bernard Tixier**
Location: **Cabrières d'Aigues, France**
Photos: **© Pere Planells**

Bathing in vines

In Wein baden

Bain dans les vignes

Bañarse en medio de las viñas

- Reinforced concrete

- Stahlbeton

- Béton armé

- Hormigón armado

House in an Old Roman Quarry

Architect: **François Privat**

Decoration: **Patricia Bradley**

Location: **Uzès, France**

Photos: © **Pere Planells**

The azure line

Der Azurblaue Strich

La ligne azur

La línea azul celeste

- Tinted cement
  Crushed stone
  Lawn

- Gefärbter Zement
  Splitt
  Rasen

- Ciment tinté
  Grava
  Gazon

- Cemento tintado
  Grava
  Césped

House in Mallorca

Design: **Rafael Calparsoro**
Location: **Mallorca, Spain**
Photos: © **Pere Planells**

A step over water
Stufe aus Wasser
Escalier d'eau
Escalón de agua

- Tinted cement
  Natural stone
  Wood from tropical forests

- Gefärbter Zement
  Naturstein
  Tropenholz

- Ciment tinté
  Pierre naturel
  Bois tropicale

- Cemento tintado
  Piedra natural
  Madera tropical

Mediterranean Zen

Architect: **Toni Esteva**

Landscape design: **Adele Juhas-Barton**

Location: **Mallorca, Spain**

Photos: © **Pere Planells**

Meditative prints in the sand
Meditative Spuren im Sand
Empreints méditatives dans le sable
Huellas meditativas en la arena

- Black mosaic tiles
  Natural stone

- Schwarze Mosaikkacheln
  Naturstein

- Mosaïque noire
  Pierre naturel

- Gresite negro
  Piedra natural

Wooden Home

Architect: **SCP d'Architectes /**
Boyer-Gibaud Percheron
Location: **Montpellier, France**
Photos: **© Pere Planells**

Dominating the landscape
Dominanz über die Landschaft
Surplombant le paysage
Dominando el paisaje

- Tinted cement
  Wood from tropical forests

- Gefärbter Zement
  Tropenholz

- Ciment tinté
  Bois tropicale

- Cemento tintado
  Madera tropical

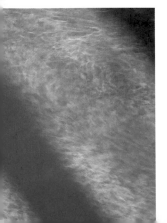

El Majal

Architect: **Karim El Achak**

Concept: **Philippe de Villegas**

Landscape design: **Jean-Charles Mazet**

Location: **Morocco**

Photos: © **Pere Planells**

In the heart of the laberynth
Im Herzen des Labyrinths
Dans le coeur du labyrinthe
En el corazón del laberinto

- Sand colour painted concrete

- Sandfarben gestrichener Beton

- Ciment peint couleur sable

- Hormigón pintado en color arena

House Chester

Architect: **Raymond Jungles**
Location: **Miami, USA**
Photos: © **Pep Escoda**

Silent guardian
Schweigsamer Hüter
Gardien silencieux
Guardián silencioso

- Black diamond-brite
  Travertine

- Schwarzes Diamond-Brite
  Travertin

- Diamond-brite en noir
  Travertin

- Diamond-brite negro
  Travertin

Palomares Residence

Architect: **Raymond Jungles**

Location: **Miami, USA**

Photos: © **Pep Escoda**

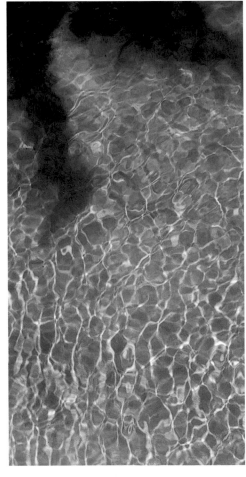

Whispering blue-green

Rauschendes Blau-Grün

Murmure bleu-vert

Azul-verde murmurando

- Marble decking
  Unpolished travertine

- Marmordeck
  Ungeglätteter Travertin

- Couverture en marbre
  Travertin non-poli

- Cubierta de mármol
  Travertin no-pulido

257

Palacio Belmonte

Design: **Frédéric Coustols**
Location: **Lisbon, Portugal**
Photos: **© Pere Planells**

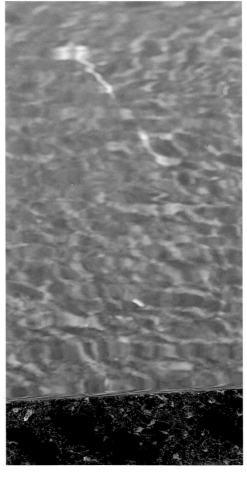

Lisbon at your feet

... und zu Füßen: Lissabon

... et à ses pieds: Lisbonne

... y a sus pies: Lisboa

- Brazilian black marble
  Teak

- Brasilianischer schwarzer Marmor
  Teakholz

- Marbre noir du Brésil
  Teck

- Mármol negro de Brasil
  Madera de teca

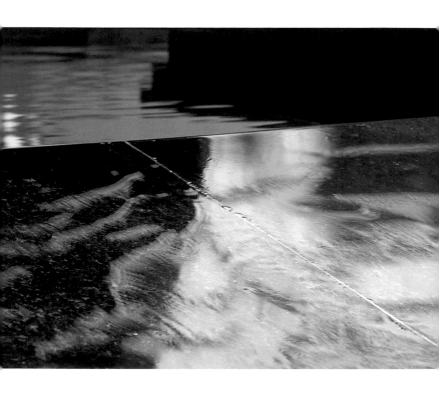

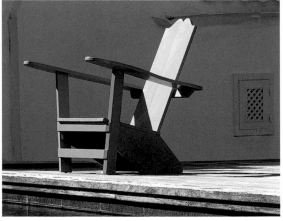

House
in Vallvidrera

Architect: **Carlos Ferrater & Joan Guibernau**

Location: **Barcelona, Spain**

Photos: © **Pere Planells**

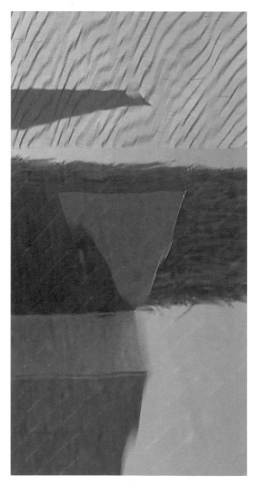

Nightswimming

Nachtbaden

Bain de minuit

Baño nocturno

- Marine-blue mosaic tiles
  Wood from tropical forests

- Marineblaue Mosaikkacheln
  Tropenholz

- Mosaïque bleu-marine
  Bois tropicale

- Gresite azul marino
  Madera tropical

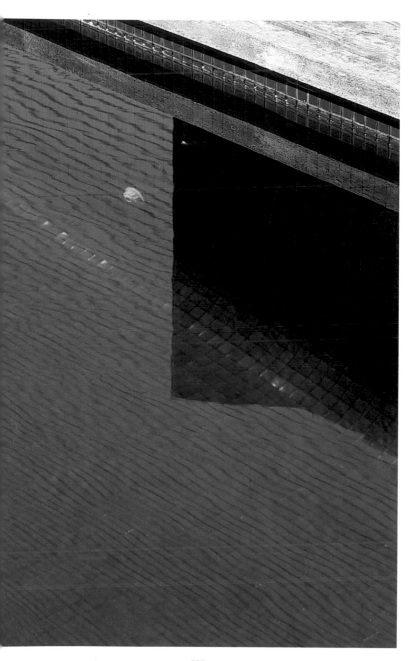

Hi Hotel

Architect: **Matali Crasset**
Location: **Nice, France**
Photos: **© Pere Planells**

Arizona on the roof

Arizona auf dem Dach

Arizona sur le toit

Arizona en el tejado

- Reinforced concrete

- Stahlbeton

- Béton armé

- Hormigón armado

Sherman Residence

Architect: **Barry Sugarman**

Location: **Miami, USA**

Photos: © **Pep Escoda**

Circular white

Kreisförmiges Weiß

Blanc circulaire

Blanco circular

- White cast Keystone (concrete)
  Marcite
  Blue ceramic
  White painted steel

- Weißer Gießbeton (Keystone)
  Marcite
  Blaue Keramikfliesen
  Weiß gestrichener Stahl

- Béton coulé blanc (Keystone)
  Marcite
  Carrelage en céramique bleue,
  Acier peint en blanc

- Hormigón proyectado (Keystone)
  Marcite
  Cerámica azul
  Acero pintado blanco

305

House Weiss

Architect: **Barry Sugarman**
Location: **Miami, USA**
Photos: **© Pep Escoda**

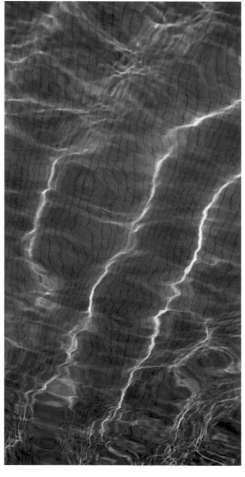

Horizontal sunbeams
Horizontale Sonnenstrahlen
Rayons de soleil horizontaux
Rayos de sol horizontales

- Marbletite
  White and yellow ceramic

- Marbletite
  Weiße und gelbe Kacheln

- Marbletite
  Céramique en blanc et jaune

- Marbletite
  Cerámica blanca y amarilla

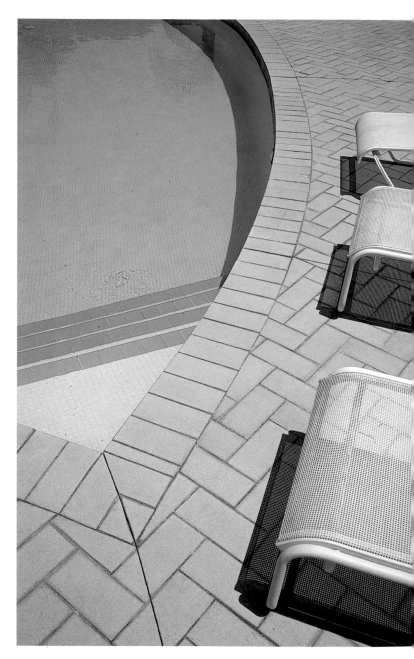

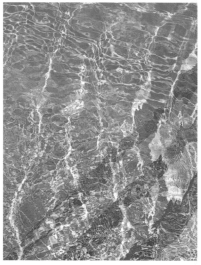

Greenwald House

Architect: **Barry Sugarman**
Location: **Miami, USA**
Photos: **© Pep Escoda**

A Pool with a view

Schwimmbad mit Aussicht

Piscine avec vue

Una piscina con vistas

- Polished concrete
  Marcite
  Blue ceramic

- Polierter Beton
  Marcite
  Blaue Keramikfliesen

- Béton poncé
  Marcite
  Carrelage en céramique bleue

- Hormigón pulido
  Marcite
  Baldosas de cerámica azul

Penzon Residence

Architect: **Luis Lozada**
Location: **Miami, USA**
Photos: © **Pep Escoda**

Elevated angles

Erhöhte Winkel

Angles élevés

Ángulos elevados

- Blue and patterned Spanish stoneware

- Blaue und gemusterte spanische Steingutfliesen

- Grès espagnole en bleu et avec dessin

- Gres español en azul y con dibujo

Barry's House Pool

Architect: **Barry Sugarman**
Location: **Miami, USA**
Photos: © **Pep Escoda**

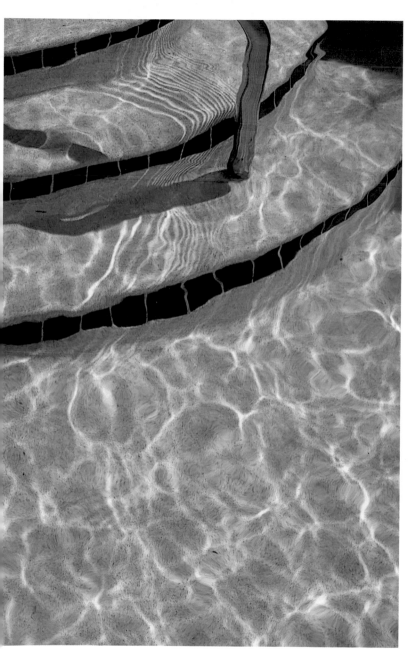

Musical water

Wassermusik

Musique acuatique

Música acuática

- Mahogany
  Marcite
  Tiles
  Stainless steel

- Mahagoni
  Marcite
  Kacheln
  Edelstahl

- Acajou
  Marcite
  Céramique
  Acier inoxidable

- Caoba
  Marcite
  Cerámica
  Acero inoxidable

In an Old Convent

Design: **María Ulecia & Javier Muñoz**
Location: **Badajoz, Spain**
Photos: **© Pere Planells**

Tuquoise light

Türkises Licht

Lumière turquoise

Luz turquesa

- Lime
  Clay
  Basketwork

- Kalk
  Ton
  Korbgeflecht

- Calcaire
  Boue
  Osier

- Cal
  Barro
  Mimbre

NATURAL POOLS

SCHWIMMTEICHE

PISCINES NATURELLES

PISCINAS NATURALES

■ Have you ever considered building a natural, completely chemical-free pool? Many of us are so conditioned to believing that all pools must be treated with chlorine or an equivalent chemical that this is a question rarely considered.

But for a moment just imagine swimming in clean, living water which doesn´t taste of chlorine and causes no skin irritation. The water in your natural pool would provide a haven for wildlife, attracting birds and small animals back into your garden.

As the benefits seem so obvious, it's surprising so few natural pools exist. Have we become so accustomed to chemically treated pools that we do not even question our preference for them, or have we actually developed a groundless fear of anything that has not been disinfected and sterilized by harsh chemicals? Some may also wonder, for example, if a natural pool would be as crystal clear as a conventional pool or if it would eventually develop algae or any other foreign substance. And so, in goes the bottle of chlorine, washing away our fears along with every other living thing in the water. After all, it may be dead and sterile, but at least its safe!

This is often as far as many of us allow our thinking to go. And yet, we only have to turn to Nature to find a possible solution. Just look at the natural purifying process happening around us all the time in rivers, streams, ponds and lakes; beautiful examples of water naturally being cleansed, oxygenated and regenerated.

Terravita Gardens, an environmentally friendly landscape gardening company in the Balearics, have given this question a lot of thought. Born and bred on the Mediterranean island of Ibiza, the three brothers who own Terravita appreciate Nature in her infinite variety and all things organic. As one of them puts it: "When I eat an apple, I'm not too bothered about how it looks or how large or glossy it is, I just want it to taste good and be good for me." So, when thinking about pool design, they were not so concerned about the water being crystal clear and azure blue as they were about its vitality and health. They were determined to develop a system that would clean the impurities without sterilizing the water and build pools that would be great to swim in.

While there are many landscape gardening companies all over Europe who have developed expertise in this area, Terravita was the first company to create natural pools in Ibiza. They have developed several tried and tested cleansing methods and are discovering which systems seem to work best in a Mediterranean climate where the challenges may be greater than in a more temperate climate.

It is important to be aware at the outset that the water balance cannot be 100% controlled and, whilst it should always be possible to see your feet, the water will not be as clear as a chemically treated pool. Suntan lotions too are not recommended. Perhaps we have been so conditioned retouched pictures in magazines and glossy fruit and vegetables on supermarket shelves, that we confuse quality with clarity. The water in a well-designed natural pool may not be crystal clear but the quality of the water in terms of life and vitality will be immeasurably superior.

There are several systems to choose from and an expert will advise which is the most suitable, depending on climate, cost and personal preference. Unlike conventional pools, natural pools do not use chemicals to sterilize the water. Instead, they attempt to emulate nature by ensuring that bacteria are filtered out and the water cleansed. It is a completely organic process.

One method, known as the technical biosystem, is to install a system of sponges which act biologically, filtering out the sediment. Effectively, you create life within the sponge by encouraging the micro organisms which live in the sponge to decompose the sediment. The water can then be passed through an ultraviolet light which prevents any floating green algae from reproducing. It does not kill the algae but keeps it well under control.

Alternatively, instead of sponges, a reedbed can be used to cleanse the water. The reeds are planted in sand gravel beds and as the water from the pool passes through the gravel larger particles are extracted. Simultaneously, the reeds and aquatic plants eat up the bacteria whilst filtering out the coarse sediment from the water. The water can then be pumped through ultra violet lights to control the algae, as mentioned above, before flowing back into the pool.

Additionally, submerged aquatics can be planted either inside the pool or in an area adjacent to the pool. These act as oxygenators, loosening and softening the water. As with most water features, especially in warmer climates, it is important to avoid creating stagnant water which can be a breeding ground for mosquitoes. The water must be kept flowing to prevent unwelcome insects. Here, fish can serve a dual purpose by helping with the water movement as well as by eating the mosquitoes!

There is no reason why all these methods should not be incorporated. In dryer climates natural pools can serve a dual purpose. For instance, Terravita Gardens, situated on an island that presents special challenges to the gardener because of the scarcity of rain, the searing summer heat and a low water table, is always happy to build balsas for their clients. The balsa will be filled with either mains or trucked in water and will be located so as to collect optimal rain water. Traditionally, balsas were and still are used for irrigation but they can also serve as a natural swimming pool if some of the methods described above are incorporated.

There is no reason why a conventional pool cannot be converted into a natural pool. The quality of water has to be experienced. Clients are frequently delighted by how soft the water feels because of the oxygenation from the aquatics.

Whether you are thinking about building a new pool or if you are an animal lover and would like to see birds and wildlife sharing your garden with you, it is worth taking time out to consider some of the benefits of having a natural pool. Swimming in living water that is completely free from chemicals and totally natural is no longer a utopia, it is easily available. Returning to the analogy of the organic apple, the difference between swimming in a chlorine pool and a natural pool is enormous; you can taste the difference! ■

NATURAL POOLS

■ Haben Sie schon einmal daran gedacht, einen natürlichen, völlig chemiefreien Swimming Pool anzulegen? Viele von uns beharren auf festgefahrenen Meinungen und glauben fest daran, dass alle Schwimmbäder mit Chlor oder anderen Chemikalien gereinigt werden müssten, so dass diese Frage nur selten gestellt wird.

Stellen Sie sich doch nur mal für einen Moment vor, in sauberem, lebendigem Wasser zu schwimmen, das nicht nach Chlor schmeckt und die Haut nicht reizt. Das Wasser in ihrem Schwimmteich wäre Anziehungspunkt für die Natur und würde Vögel und andere kleine Tiere zurück in ihren Garten bringen.

Da die Vorteile so offen auf der Hand liegen, ist es um so erstaunlicher, dass es bisher erst so wenige Schwimmteiche gibt. Sind wir so sehr an chemisch behandelte Pools gewöhnt, dass wir nicht einmal über diese Vorliebe nachdenken? Oder haben wir gar eine irrationale Furcht entwickelt vor allem, das nicht durch scharfe Chemikalien desinfiziert und keimfrei gemacht wurde? Einige mögen sich beispielsweise auch fragen, ob ein Schwimmteich ebenso kristallklar wie ein herkömmlicher Pool sei, oder ob sich eventuell Algen oder fremde Substanzen bilden könnten. So wird schnell zur Flasche mit dem Chlor gegriffen und unsere Bedenken zusammen mit allem anderen Lebendigen im Wasser ausgelöscht. Es kann schließlich tot und steril sein, aber immerhin ist es sicher!

Oft denken wir gar nicht weiter drüber nach. Dennoch reicht ein Blick in die Natur, um mögliche Alternativen zu finden. Sehen Sie sich doch den natürlich ablaufenden Reinigungsprozess an, der ständig um uns herum abläuft, in Flüssen, Bächen, Teichen und Seen; wunderbare Beispiele für Wasser, das auf natürliche Art und Weise gereinigt, mit Sauerstoff angereichert und regeneriert wird.

Terravita Gardens, ein umweltfreundliches Landschaftsgärtner-Unternehmen auf den Balearen, hat sich ausgiebig diesem Thema gewidmet. Auf Ibiza geboren und aufgewachsen schätzen die drei Brüder, das das Unternehmen gegründet haben, die Natur und alles Organische. Einer von ihnen drückt es so aus: „Wenn ich einen Apfel esse, geht es mir weniger darum, wie groß oder glänzend er ist, sondern ich möchte einfach, dass er gut schmeckt und gut für mich ist." Daher richten die drei ihr Augenmerk beim Pool-Design nicht so sehr auf kristallklares und azurblaues Wasser, sondern vielmehr auf Lebendigkeit und Gesundheit. Sie beschlossen, ein System zu entwickeln, das die Verunreinigungen säubern würde, ohne das Wasser zu sterilisieren, und Swimming Pools zu bauen, in denen zu schwimmen ein Genuss ist.

Verschiedene Landschaftsplanungsbüros in ganz Europa haben sich zu Fachleuten auf diesem Gebiet entwickelt. Terravita war jedoch die erste Firma, die Schwimmteiche auf Ibiza anlegte. Sie hat verschiedene erprobte und geprüfte Filtermethoden entwickelt und erforscht auch weiterhin, welche Systeme im mediterranen Klima am besten funktionieren, was vielleicht eine größere Herausforderung darstellt als in gemäßigteren Breiten.

Es ist wichtig, sich darüber klar zu werden, dass zu Anfang das Gleichgewicht des Wassers nicht zu 100% kontrolliert werden kann und dass, auch wenn man immer die eigenen Füße sehen können sollte, das Wasser nicht so durchsichtig sein wird, wie ein chemisch gereinigter Pool. Sonnenschutzmittel sind ebenfalls nicht zu empfehlen. Anscheinend wurden wir durch retuschierte Bilder in Zeitschriften und durch glänzendes Obst und Gemüse in den Regalen der Supermärkte darauf getrimmt, Qualität mit Reinheit zu verwechseln. Das Wasser in einem gut geplanten Schwimmteich mag also nicht kristallklar sein, die Wasserqualität ist im Hinblick auf Leben und Lebendigkeit jedoch unvergleichlich höher.

Verschiedene Methoden bieten sich zur Wasseraufbereitung an; ein Fachmann wird je nach Klima, Budget und persönlichen Wünschen zum Passenden raten. Im Gegensatz zu herkömmlichen Pools benutzen Schwimmteiche keinerlei Chemikalien, um das Wasser zu sterilisieren. Stattdessen setzen sie darauf, die Natur nachzuahmen und sicher zu stellen, dass Bakterien ausgefiltert und das Wasser gereinigt wird. Es ist ein vollkommen organischer Prozess.

Eine Methode, das sogenannte technische Biosystem, besteht darin, eine Schwammkultur anzusiedeln, die rein biologisch arbeitet und die Sedimente ausfiltert. Man kann effektvoll Leben schaffen, indem man die Mikroorganismen anregt, die im Schwamm leben, die Sedimente abzubauen. Danach kann das Wasser mit ultraviolettem Licht bestrahlt werden, das sämtliche schwimmende Grünalgen an der Verbreitung hindert. Es tötet die Algen nicht ab, aber hält sie unter Kontrolle.

Alternativ kann statt Schwämmen auch ein Rietgrasbeet zum Einsatz kommen. Das Riet wird in Sand-Kiesbeete gepflanzt, und größere Schwebstoffe werden aus dem Wasser entfernt, wenn es aus dem Pool durch die Granulatschichten sickert. Gleichzeitig zersetzen das Riet und andere Wasserpflanzen die Bakterien, während sie die groben Sedimente ausfiltern. Das Wasser kann dann an ultraviolettem Licht vorbeigepumpt werden, damit – wie zuvor beschrieben – der Algenwuchs begrenzt wird, bevor das Wasser in den Pool zurückfließt.

Zusätzlich können Wasserpflanzen im Pool oder in einem an das Becken angrenzenden Bereich gepflanzt werden. Sie wirken als Sauerstofflieferanten und machen das Wasser weicher. Wie bei den meisten Wasserstellen ist es, besonders in den wärmeren Klimazonen, wichtig, stehendes Wasser zu vermeiden, das eine Brutstätte für Mücken sein kann. Das Wasser muss beständig fließen, um nicht-willkommenen Insekten vorzubeugen. Fische können hierbei einen zweifachen Nutzen erfüllen, einerseits indem sie das Wasser bewegen, andererseits indem sie die Mücken fressen!

Es gibt keinen Grund, nicht alle diese Methoden anzuwenden. In trockeneren Gebieten können Schwimmteiche einen zusätzlichen Nutzen erfüllen. Terravita Gardens, auf einer Insel ansässig, die aufgrund der geringen Regenfälle, der stechenden Sommerhitze und des niedrigen Grundwasserpegels eine besondere Herausforderung für den Gärtner darstellt, ist stets daran interessiert, Wasserspeicher für ihre Kunden zu bauen. Das Reservoir wird entweder mit Wasser aus der Leitung oder per LKW herbeigeschafftem Wasser gefüllt und so angelegt, dass Regenwasser optimal aufgefangen wird. Traditionell dienen diese Speicher zur Bewässerung, aber sie können auch als natürlicher Swimming Pool dienen, wenn einige der oben genannten Methoden zum Einsatz kommen.

Es gibt keinen Grund dafür, warum ein herkömmlicher Swimming Pool nicht in einen Schwimmteich umgestaltet werden kann. Man muss die Wasserqualität einfach erfahren haben. Viele Kunden sind häufig besonders erfreut darüber, wie weich sich das Wasser anfühlt, dank der Sauerstoffanreicherung durch die Wasserpflanzen.

Ob Sie daran denken, einen neuen Pool anzulegen oder ob Sie ein Tierliebhaber sind, der seinen Garten mit Vögeln und anderen Tierarten teilen möchte, es lohnt sich, in Ruhe über die Vorteile eines natürlichen Swimming Pools nachzudenken. In lebendigem Wasser zu schwimmen, das absolut chemiefrei und natürlich ist, ist nicht länger Utopie, sondern einfach zu verwirklichen. Um auf das Bild des biologischen Apfels zurückzukommen; der Unterschied zwischen einem gechlorten Pool und einem Schwimmteich ist enorm: Man kann ihn schmecken! ∎

SCHWIMMTEICHE

■ Avez-vous déjà pensé à construire une piscine naturelle, sans aucun élément chimique? Nous sommes pour la plupart tellement conditionnés à croire que les piscines doivent être traitées avec du chlore, ou un équivalent chimique, que cette question entre rarement en ligne de compte.

Mais imaginez-vous, l'espace d'un instant, nageant dans une onde claire et limpide n'ayant pas le goût du chlore et ne vous irritant pas la peau. L'eau de votre piscine naturelle serait un paradis pour la vie sauvage, attirant oiseaux et petits animaux dans votre jardin.

Les avantages sont si évidents que la rareté des piscines naturelles apparaît surprenante. Sommes-nous si habitués aux piscines traitées chimiquement que nous ne questionnions plus nos préférences? Ou avons-nous développé une peur infondée envers tout ce qui n'est pas désinfecté et stérilisé par des produits chimiques agressifs? Il est également loisible de se demander si, par exemple, une piscine naturelle serait aussi limpide qu'une piscine conventionnelle, ou si elle serait prône à développer des algues ou autres substances étrangères... La petite bouteille de chlore fait sa réapparition, emportant avec elle nos peurs ainsi que toute autre forme de vie. Après tout, elle peut être morte et stérile mais elle est sûre.

Nos pensées ne s'aventurent, assez souvent, pas plus loin. Et pourtant, il suffit de se tourner vers Mère Nature pour trouver une solution possible. Observons simplement les nombreux processus de purification naturels nous entourant en permanence dans les rivières, torrents, étangs et lacs : de superbes exemples d'eau purifiée, oxygénée et régénérée naturellement.

Terravita Gardens, une société de jardiniers paysagistes, responsable écologiquement, des Baléares s'est longuement interrogé sur la question. Nés et élevés sur l'île méditerranéenne d'Ibiza, les trois frères propriétaires de Terravita apprécient la Nature dans son infinie variété et l'ensemble de la faune et de la flore. Comme l'a déclaré l'un d'eux : « Lorsque je mange une pomme, ce qui m'intéresse ce n'est pas son apparence, si elle grosse ou brillante. Je veux seulement qu'elle ait bon goût et qu'elle me fasse du bien. » Dès lors, dans le cadre de leur réflexion sur le design de piscines, ils étaient moins intéressés par la clarté cristalline et le bleu azuré de l'eau que par sa vitalité et son effet sur la santé. Ils étaient déterminés à développer un système qui pourrait nettoyer les impuretés sans stériliser l'eau et à créer des piscines où il ferait bon nager.

Bien que de nombreuses entreprises de jardiniers paysagistes en Europe aient développé une expertise dans ce domaine, Terravita fut la première à créer des piscines naturelles à Ibiza. La société a développé plusieurs méthodes de nettoyage, testées encore et encore, et découvre quels systèmes semblent donner les meilleurs résultats sous un climat méditerranéen, le défi pouvant s'avérer plus ardu que sous des latitudes plus tempérées.

Il est important de prendre conscience, dès le départ, que l'équilibre de l'eau ne peut être contrôlé à 100 % et, bien qu'il soit toujours possible de voir ses pieds, l'eau ne sera pas aussi claire que celle d'une piscine traitée chimiquement. Les lotions solaires sont également déconseillées. Peut-être avons-nous été conditionnés si profondément par les images retouchées de fruits et de légumes brillants aux étalages des supermarchés dans les magazines que nous en sommes venu à confondre clarté et qualité. L'eau d'une piscine bien conçue n'aura peut-être pas une clarté cristalline mais ses qualités en termes de vie et de vitalité seront incommensurablement supérieures.

Plusieurs systèmes s'offrent à votre choix et un expert vous conseillera sur le mieux adapté, selon le climat, le coût et vos préférences personnelles. Contrairement aux piscines conventionnelles, les piscines naturelles n'utilisent aucun produit chimique pour stériliser l'eau. En lieu et place, elles essayent d'imiter la nature en assurant que les bactéries sont filtrées et l'eau nettoyée. C'est un processus complètement organique.

Une méthode – connue comme le biosystème technique – passe par l'installation d'un système d'éponges qui filtrent les sédiments biologiquement. Dans les faits, vous créez la vie dans l'éponge en encourageant les micro-organismes y vivant à décomposer les sédiments. L'eau peut alors passer sous une lumière aux ultra-violets qui évite la reproduction de toute algue verte flottante. Sans les tuer, elle les gardent sous controle strict.

Les roseaux constituent une alternative aux éponges pour nettoyer l'eau. Les roseaux sont plantés dans un lit de gravier sablonneux et, l'eau de la piscine traversant le gravier, les particules les plus importantes sont extraites. Simultanément, les roseaux et les plantes aquatiques s'alimentent des bactéries tout en filtrant les sédiments grossiers hors de l'eau. L'eau peut alors être pompée pour passer sous des rayons ultra-violets pour contrôler les algues, comme mentionné précédemment, avant de revenir dans la piscine.

Par ailleurs, des plantes aquatiques immergées peuvent être plantées soit dans la piscine ou dans une zone adjacente. Elles se comportent comme des générateurs d'oxygène, libérant et adoucissant l'eau. Une caractéristique de l'eau, spécialement sous des climats plus chauds : il est important d'éviter de créer des eaux stagnantes, un foyer de développement pour les moustiques. L'eau doit continuer à circuler pour éviter les insectes importuns. Ici, le poisson peut servir un double propos en participant au mouvement de l'eau tout en dévorant les moustiques.

Aucune raison n'empêche toutes ces méthodes d'être incorporées ensemble. Sous les climats secs, les piscines naturelles ont un double objet. Ainsi, Terravita Gardens, située sur une île présentant des défis nombreux pour le jardinier en raison du rationnement de l'eau, de la chaleur estivale et d'une nappe phréatique faible, est toujours ravi de créer des réservoirs pour ses clients. Ils seront remplis d'eau courante, ou apportée par camion, et disposés afin de collecter de manière optimale les eaux de pluie. Traditionnellement, les réservoirs ont été utilisés et servent encore à l'irrigation. Mais ils peuvent également se transformer en piscine naturelle si certaines des méthodes décrites auparavant sont intégrées.

Aucune raison ne s'oppose, par ailleurs, à la conversion d'une piscine conventionnelle en piscine naturelle. La qualité de l'eau est une expérience nécessaire. Les clients sont souvent enthousiasmés par la douceur de l'eau, en raison de l'oxygénation par les plantes aquatiques.

Que vous pensiez à construire une nouvelle piscine ou que vous soyez un fan de la vie animale et souhaitiez voir oiseaux et petits animaux partager votre jardin avec vous, il faut prendre le temps de considérer les avantages offerts par une piscine naturelle. Nager dans une eau vivante, libre de tout produit chimique et parfaitement naturelle, n'est plus une utopie mais bien à portée de la main. Revenant à l'analogie de la pomme biologique, la différence entre une piscine chlorée et une piscine naturelle est énorme : savourez-la ! ■

PISCINES NATURELLES

■ ¿Ha pensado alguna vez en tener una piscina natural completamente libre de sustancias químicas? Muchas personas están tan condicionadas por la creencia de que el agua de las piscinas con cloro o alguna sustancia similar debe tratarse, que ni siquiera se plantean esta posibilidad.

Imagine por un momento que está nadando en agua limpia y viva, sin sabor a cloro, que no le irrita la piel. El agua de su piscina natural podría constituir además un refugio para la vida salvaje, que atrae a los pájaros y otros pequeños animales a su jardín.

Aunque las ventajas parecen tan obvias, sorprende las pocas piscinas naturales que existen. ¿Estamos tan acostumbrados a las piscinas tratadas químicamente que no nos cuestionamos si nos gustan? ¿O es que hemos desarrollado un irracional miedo a todo aquello que no esté desinfectado y esterilizado con productos químicos agresivos? A algunos les preocuparía, por ejemplo, el hecho de que el agua de una piscina natural no sea tan cristalina como la de una convencional, o que se desarrollen algas o algún otro organismo extraño. De esta manera, con la botella de cloro limpiarían sus miedos junto a cualquier otro rastro de vida. Puede que el resultado sea un medio muerto y estéril, pero proporciona un desenlace seguro.

Este suele ser el razonamiento de la mayoría. Pero la naturaleza nos ofrece otras muchas posibles respuestas. Tan solo tenemos que observar el proceso natural de purificación del agua de nuestros ríos, corrientes, charcas y lagos; hermosos ejemplos de agua limpia, oxigenada y regenerada por medios naturales.

Terravita Gardens, una compañía de diseño paisajista ecológico de las Islas Baleares, se ha planteado largo tiempo esta cuestión. Nacidos y criados en la isla mediterránea de Ibiza, los tres hermanos propietarios de Terravita aprecian la naturaleza en su infinita variedad y con todos sus elementos orgánicos. Según las palabras de uno de ellos: "Cuando como una manzana no miro si es grande y de aspecto brillante, solo quiero que tenga un buen sabor y que sea sana". Por ello, en lo referente al diseño de piscinas no les preocupa tanto que el agua esté clara como el cristal y presente el característico color azul cielo, sino la vitalidad y salubridad del medio. Por esta razón, decidieron desarrollar un sistema que eliminara las impurezas sin necesidad de esterilizar el agua, y que resultara un verdadero placer nadar en ella.

Aunque muchas de las compañías de diseño paisajista de toda Europa tienen especialistas en ese campo, Terravita fue la primera que creó piscinas naturales en Ibiza. Esta sociedad ha descubierto, después de experimentar y desarrollar muchos métodos de purificación, qué sistemas son los más eficientes en el área mediterránea donde los retos son mayores que en otras zonas de climas más moderados.

El balance del agua no puede controlarse en un 100%; aunque siempre pueda uno verse los pies, el agua de una piscina natural nunca estará tan clara como la de una piscina tratada químicamente. Tampoco será posible bañarse con loción bronceadora. Quizá estemos tan condicionados por los anuncios de las revistas y la fruta tratada y brillante de los supermercados que confundimos calidad con claridad. El agua en las piscinas naturales bien diseñadas puede no ser totalmente cristalina, pero su calidad en términos de vida y vitalidad será infinitamente mejor.

Hay muchos sistemas para elegir y los expertos nos ayudarán a decidirnos por el más recomendable, dependiendo del clima, el coste y las preferencias personales. A diferencia de las piscinas convencionales, en las naturales no se utilizan productos químicos para esterilizar el agua. En su lugar, se emula la naturaleza, gracias a la infiltración de las bacterias en el agua que aseguran una total limpieza. El proceso es completamente orgánico.

Uno de los métodos más habituales, conocido como "biosistema técnico", consiste en instalar un procedimiento de esponjas que actúa biológicamente y filtra los sedimentos. De esta forma, se crea vida ya que se estimulan los microorganismos que viven en ellas para que descompongan los sedimentos. Posteriormente, el agua se somete a la acción de rayos ultravioleta que impiden la reproducción de las algas verdes flotantes. No se trata de destruir las algas, sino de mantener su población bajo control.

Otra alternativa para la higiene del agua es la utilización de juncales en lugar de esponjas. Los juncos o cañas se plantan en lechos de grava y arena, de forma que cuando el agua de la piscina circula por ellos, la partículas más grandes se filtran. Al mismo tiempo, los juncos y la plantas acuáticas acaban con las bacterias cuando filtran los sedimentos flotantes más gruesos. Entonces, el agua se bombea antes de ser devuelta a la piscina para que fluya a través de los rayos ultravioleta y, de esta manera, controlar la reproducción de las algas tal y como se ha mencionado arriba.

Además, las plantas acuáticas submarinas se pueden plantar dentro de la piscina o en un área adyacente. Estas actúan como elemento de oxigenación, que relaja y suaviza el agua. Es muy importante, especialmente en climas cálidos, evitar las aguas estancadas que atraen a los mosquitos; el agua debe fluir constantemente para prevenir la presencia de insectos indeseados. En este proceso, los peces desarrollan una doble función crucial ya que agitan el agua y devoran los mosquitos.

Ninguna razón impide aplicar esos métodos. En climas muy secos, el agua puede tener además diversas utilidades. Por ejemplo, la empresa Terravita Gardens, ubicada en una isla que presenta especiales retos a la jardinería debido a la escasez de lluvia, el abrasador calor del verano y el bajo nivel de aguas freáticas, satisface a sus clientes con la construcción de balsas. Estas, alimentadas con agua transportada por tuberías o en cisternas, se construyen para que actúen como recolectoras de agua de lluvia. Tradicionalmente, estas embarcaciones se vienen utilizando para la irrigación, pero también pueden servir de piscina natural si se aplican algunos de los métodos ya indicados.

No existe ninguna razón para que una piscina convencional no pueda convertirse en una natural. La calidad del agua debe ser comprobada. Los clientes, generalmente, quedan encantados con el perfil suave del agua oxigenada por las plantas acuáticas.

Si está pensando en construir una nueva piscina o si es amante de los animales y le gustaría ver como los pájaros y la vida salvaje comparten su jardín, debería considerar las ventajas de tener una piscina natural. Nadar en aguas vivas, libres por completo de productos químicos y totalmente naturales ya no es una utopía, sino algo sencillo y factible. Basta con recordar la analogía de la manzana no tratada; la diferencia entre nadar en una piscina clorada y una natural es enorme. Se trata de una cuestión de gusto. ◼

PISCINAS NATURALES

Green Countryside

Design: **Terravita Gardens**

Location: **Ibiza, Spain**

Photos: © **Pere Planells**

Blooming cascades
Blühende Kaskaden
Cascades en fleur
Cascadas en flor

- Gunited concrete
  Natural colors
  Big rocks

- Spritzbeton
  Naturfarben
  Felsbrocken

- Béton projeté
  Couleurs naturelles
  Gros rochers

- Hormigón proyectado
  Colores naturales
  Rocas

House in Ibiza

Design: **Terravita Gardens**
Location: **Ibiza, Spain**
Photos: **© Pere Planells**

Rooted water

Verwurzeltes Wasser

Eau de souches

Agua arraigada

- Gunited concrete
  Natural colors
  Big rocks

- Spritzbeton
  Naturfarben
  Felsbrocken

- Béton projeté
  Couleurs naturelles
  Gros rochers

- Hormigón proyectado
  Colores naturales
  Rocas

GRATEFULLY
DANKSAGUNG
REMERCIEMENTS
AGRADECIMIENTOS

Antoinette Alain Houtsaeger

Yacquelinis Alan

Mr. & Mrs. Bradley

Christophe Ceard

Coconut Company. Palma de Mallorca

Eric & Lawrence, "Le Jas de l'Ange"

Gandia Blasco S.A. Ontinyent (Valencia)

Chris Lawrence, "The Best of Morocco"

Beatriz Maximo

Neus & Gilbert

Françoise Pialoux

Kamila Regent & Pierre Jaccaud, "Chambre de Séjour avec Vue..."

Emmanuel Stahn

Toni & Lala

Maria Ulecia & Javier Muñoz, "Convento La Parra"

Jérôme Vermen & Michel Durand-Meyrier, "La Cour des Mirtes"

Philippe de Villegas

Other Designpocket titles by teNeues:

Asian Interior Design 3-8238-4527-6

Bathroom Design 3-8238-4523-3

Berlin Apartments 3-8238-5596-4

Cafés & Restaurants 3-8238-5478-X

Cool Hotels 3-8238-5556-5

Cosmopolitan Hotels 3-8238-4546-2

Country Hotels 3-8238-5574-3

Exhibition Design 3-8238-5548-4

Furniture/Möbel/Meubles/Muebles Design 3-8238-5575-1

Garden Design 3-8238-4524-1

Italian Interior Design 3-8238-5495-X

Kitchen Design 3-8238-4522-5

London Apartments 3-8238-5558-1

Los Angeles Houses 3-8238-5594-8

Miami Houses 3-8238-4545-4

New York Apartments 3-8238-5557-3

Office Design 3-8238-5578-6

Paris Apartments 3-8238-5571-9

Product Design 3-8238-5597-2

San Francisco Houses 3-8238-4526-8

Showrooms 3-8238-5496-8

Ski Hotels 3-8238-4543-8

Spa & Wellness Hotels 3-8238-5595-6

Staircases 3-8238-5572-7

Sydney Houses 3-8238-4525-X

Tokyo Houses 3-8238-5573-5

Tropical Houses 3-8238-4544-6

Each volume:

12.5 x 18.5 cm
400 pages
c. 400 color illustrations